# Forgive
# Forget
# FORWARD

*By Katherine D. Carey*

*Forgive, Forget, FORWARD*
Published by Leading Through Living Community LLC

Copyright © 2015 by Katherine D. Carey

ISBN-10:  0-9891457-9-4
ISBN-13:  978-0-9891457-9-4

Cover picture and design by Joshe Martin

Scripture quotations are from the Holy Bible - www.Bible.com

For information:
Leading Through Living Community LLC
6790 W. Broad Street Suite 300
Douglasville, GA 30135

# Acknowledgements

I give all my Honor and Glory to GOD for putting this heavily on my heart to write. Sometimes we have to stop and listen to understand what He is telling us to do, and once I did that, I had the answer to my purpose and this book is the result.

I also thank Jerry Cowell, brother in Christ, colleague and friend who had no idea this was on me to write, but while having a conversation said to me, "You need to write a book." That was confirmation from GOD to continue what I had started.

I also wish to thank those people who have mistreated me, talked about me, used me and just wanted to see me fail. Although those actions were not made in love, the Holy Spirit transformed that negative energy into positive motivation, and pushed me to write when I was tired.

Last but never least, I thank my family and true friends. My brothers are so awesome with all they have done for me over the years. They are my ROCK and I appreciate and love them so much. I thank GOD for them. He knows how to put a family together, because I cannot imagine my life without them and the many lessons they have taught me.

So Thank You.

# Interlude

I hope you will enjoy my story, thoughts and opinion.... And just so you will know during the time I'm writing this I'm also going through a breakup. This has been the worst one because I thought with all my heart he was my soul mate. You know I think there will only be one time in your life when you meet that person and you know from the bottom of your heart that this is *the* man that GOD has designed for you, and he will feel the same way.

Breakups hurt, especially when "we" think this is the man for us... but is he really? And how do we know? Here are my thoughts on how to answer these questions. I hope they help.

# Table of Contents

# Are You Happy?

This should be one of the first questions we ask ourselves. We normally ask ourselves something like this: "If I'm happy with everything that is going on, then I'm ok." But I think we should look a little deeper than that.

Being happy means you are satisfied completely with everything in your life. You can honestly say you wake up with a smile and go to bed with one. You don't let anything bother you, and life is just _good_.

The Webster's definition of happy is "feeling pleasure and enjoyment because of your life, situation, etc.
        -showing or causing feelings of pleasure and enjoyment
        -pleased or glad about a particular situation, event, etc."

Now, if you can honestly say this is you and how you feel about your situation, then you are okay. However, if there are other things on your mind and you are stressing, then you may not be completely happy and it's probably time to do something about it.

It has been on me for a while now to write something. I hope this will help you deal with whatever situation you are going through.

I am not a psychologist or psychiatrist, but I write from life and my personal experience. The purpose of this is to let you know that <u>you are not alone</u>. You are not the only one going through something. We all feel a certain" way", depending on what is going on in our lives at that time. I have learned to pay attention to those feelings, and I learn to do better from those experiences, situations, and relationships.

Sometimes when I am dealing with issues, I don't understand why they are happening or how I'm going to get past them. Personally, relationship and financial situations seem to be the hardest to deal with. Break-ups are especially hard to deal with when you really love "that person"...

I'm now in my 40's and have never been married. Most will probably say. "It will never happen now." And I think for the most part I'm okay with that. I've had some good and bad relationships and I've learned from each.

You may think there's something wrong with me because I can't get a husband or keep a man. Well, at one time I thought maybe there was. But after my last relationship, I've realized that it's okay either way if I marry or not because I'm happy being in relationship with _me_.

Before my last relationship, I'd always said I was born Katherine Carey and this was the name I'd die with. Well, I've changed my mind about that. Now I think that who is meant for me will be for me and if I find the man to marry at my age then it will be worth it. If not, then I wasn't meant to be married.

Life is full of trials and challenges, and it took me a while to acknowledge that. I've heard it before and never really thought about it until I was really going through something. My last break up hurt me to my heart in a way I never thought was possible. So that tells you that this was a love like no other. I just knew this was the man GOD had designed for me. Once I read Steve Harvey's book Act Like A Lady, Think Like A Man", I knew he was the man for me. I prayed for him, and during my prayers I described all the qualities I wanted him to have. And once we were introduced and I got to know "him", I knew he was the one... or so I thought.

We had the physical attraction, he was financially secure, a really nice person, and my family loved him from day one. Oh, did I mention he was a product of Steve Harvey's book? I received my first ring within five months. Although it wasn't an engagement ring, it was a ring stating that he loved me and I wasn't wasting my time...

But after two-and-a-half years, our relationship changed and I didn't know why. I just knew that he had became someone I didn't recognize. He completely changed. I tried to understand and give him space, but I was completely in the dark to the things that were going on around me... and I had no idea about the woman because it seemed as if we were always together. I was so confident in my relationship that I didn't worry about anything. We were happy and in love, and spent a lot of time together. We were only apart when he did his "guy thing" or just needed quality alone-time, which I didn't mind because I enjoyed mine as well.

Yet out of nowhere, he seemed to distance himself from me. Why? I had no idea. And to this day he has never given me an explanation as to what happen or why things changed. When I tried to talk with him about it, he'd just reply that it was him or he'd be dishonest. Eventually, he just left. The lack of closure led me to dwell and linger on the breakup for years.

Until now.

# Sharing My Experiences

*Growing Up*

When I was a teenager, I often wanted freedom to do the things other kids did, and could not understand why my dad was so hard on me. I just thought he was a mean man. I really did! I thought this man did not want me to have fun or be able to hang out like my brothers. It was okay for him to hang out with his friends and have fun, but with me everything was limited. I didn't understand why I was not allowed to have a boyfriend. When I was 16 I was allowed to have a friend over, but we had to be in the house, specifically and living room. It was no fun, but I appreciated at least being able to do that.

Years later, I called my dad out of the blue one day and told him how much I appreciated him being so strict during my formative years because that shaped me to be the person I am today. Because I wasn't running around town, getting into all kinds of "situations", and was able to focus on family and my career has led me to this place of peace in my life. The fact that I have lived in the same town all my life and people still ask me where I'm from is amazing. This place is not that big and if it was not for Fort Benning, our town wouldn't be the size it is.

*Career*

We often don't understand, especially girls, why our parents are so hard on us. But let me say they are looking out for us. Don't rebel, just go with it and try to understand. For my young sisters out there, trust me when I say you *will* appreciate and understand it all when you get older! Don't get me wrong: I think when you're a teenager you should have fun and enjoy life. But once you graduate from high school, it's time to make choices: college, military or a job. Whatever you decide to do, please have a plan and make it happen. Today is a lot different than when I grew up. No one pushed me to do anything, so I ended up working job after job having no idea what I wanted to do in life. I want so much more for my young sisters...

*Realizations*
I want to share some of the things that have been done to me over the years and I hope this will help you to understand that you are not the only one who has experience these things. It's important that you know that you are not only a survivor, but a conqueror, and that you will get through these things!

When I was going through my relationship drama and trauma, I would always think:
-"Why is this happening to me?"
-"Why am I getting mistreated?"
-"I'm a good person, I have been nothing but faithful and honest, why me?"
-"What did I do to deserve this?"
-"I've always been good, yet I keep getting mistreated! Why?!"

My relationships have all lasted about five years. I didn't realize that until I hit 40 and my last relationship had been over for about a year. At that time, I was really going through something because once again, I had been dumped and mistreated by another man. The last three relationships, I was cheated on and told that it was because "other women were willing to do what I wasn't." That's hurtful, but true. I have standards and I'm not going to change those to please anyone. Sometimes we can get caught up pleasing someone else and we forget about self. We are the most important. These are our lives and we have to be happy!

*Standards*

One standard I strictly adhere to is if it doesn't feel right and I don't like it then, I say no. If he cares about me and really wants to be with me, he will understand and respect me. If he can't accept me for who I am, then he doesn't deserve me in the first place. It took me a while to "get it", but eventually I did - and there was no turning back.

I have to be honest and say that there were times that I went there and tried things that I didn't care for just to please a person, but it's wasn't for me and I couldn't pretend that it was. And yes, I'm speaking on sexual things. Some men seem to think it's selfish because you won't have oral sex with them, but really it's a personal choice. And let me be clear: I'm upfront from the beginning about what I'm not into. If he is into this and willing to perform on me, that's his personal choice and he should still respect mine.

*Ladies you don't have to do anything you don't want to.* Always value yourself and know your worth. Never do something that makes you feel uncomfortable, or do something because your guy says, "If you love me you will". Really?! No! If he loves you he understands and respects your standards. Because believe you me, that even if you do whatever it is he has asked, that alone will not stop him from cheating on you, disrespecting, you and leaving you. He has to want to stay, want to be faithful, want to love and cherish you.

Now be clear: when I marry, I will definitely make adjustments and do things for my *husband*. I think that a woman should do what pleases her husband and he should do the same. That is a true commitment and you share certain things with only each other. And wouldn't it be good to say, "I've done this only with my husband?" Yes, I think it will.

Getting to know someone as a friend first, especially if there is a connection, will make for a lasting relationship. This allows time to discuss your likes and dislikes with your friend. One thing is for sure: if it doesn't work out, you will have a friend, and you're not regretting another relationship that didn't work.

## *Trying Things Out*

I was looking for something different from the men I had dated in the past, but just didn't have any direction. So I dated, but nothing serious. I went on dates with people even when I knew nothing would come of it. I had a "friend with benefits" situation for a little while, too. And that's because we had an understanding. Now, if you decide to have that type of relationship, make sure there is an understanding. Make sure this is a friend, he wants the same thing, and neither of you get your feelings involved. When you have a "friend with benefits" situation, please understand it's just that. You're not ready for a relationship and neither is he. Keep your feelings under control. One way to do that is not to spend a lot of time together. You hook up and "keep it moving". Always practice safe sex. I will say that everything walking and looking good doesn't mean it is. Although I took the "friends with benefits" route, I wouldn't do it again. I didn't like the casualness of the encounters, and really wanted something real and tangible - a true relationship.

## *Self-Awareness*

What's really made me think about my life - the decisions I've made and situations I've allowed myself to get into - stem from my last relationship.

I've only had 4 serious relationships in my life. The last one put me on my knees so many nights crying for what seemed like forever that I actually thought I was losing control. I had lost focus on a lot of things, and trying to keep it under control at times was really hard. I tried to hide my feelings, the failing of the relationship from family and friends because this was the man I thought GOD had designed just for me. He broke my heart and I just couldn't figure out how to get it or him back. It's been a very painful journey. When your heart is broken and the pain is almost unbearable, that's some serious love. Some people may say "get over it and move on", but that's easier said than done. When it's your heart, it hurts and this one cut me deep.

Eventually you get past the hurt and pain, but it's a process getting there. Nothing happens over night.

# My Story

We've all heard the saying "what goes around comes around". I think there is some truth to this saying, but I'm trying to figure out why this heartbreak came around to me. I know that sometimes we go through things for various reasons, but I still want to know why this happened to *me?*

## *Meet "Him"*

My relationship with "him" started in 2009. We met through a mutual friend. The relationship started good from the first day we met. We exchanged numbers and he called me that night to make sure I made it home safely. We met the next day at the park and talked a little, just spending time together getting to know each other. This went on for a few weeks. We went to dinner, the movies, clubs - there was no limit to what we would try and there was nothing to hide.

We saw each other every day after work and even on the weekends. There was never any indication that he was in another relationship. He told me he was not and for me that was enough. Also, the person who introduced us verified this before the introduction because she knows the type of person I am: she specifically told "him" that I don't do or like drama. I mentioned this to him as well - no games. I asked for honesty and communication from the beginning.

There was definitely a connection between us immediately, and he was very respectful and nice toward me. He never tried anything when we were getting to know each other. I spent the night with him, usually on the weekends, and he respected my boundaries and the fact that I would not have sex with him because we had not agreed on a committed relationship. I also hadn't brought him to my home or around my children because at the time, my children were all teenagers - my oldest son had graduated, but I had one in high school and a daughter in middle school.

About a month into our "getting to know you" phase, he asked me to be his woman - a committed "us only" relationship. I accepted, and from that moment on we were a couple.

After a couple of months I finally let him meet my children. I also took him to Atlanta to meet my family and then to my hometown Waycross, Georgia to meet the rest. Everyone loved him (but in retrospect, maybe they just happy to see me finally bring someone home). Not everyone gets to meet the family. Of my four serious relationships, only two have met the family and he was the second. He took me to meet his mom, and so I was thinking, "I'm meeting mother, he really likes me!" Most men have to really be into you when you met their mom... I also met the rest of his family.

*Enjoy "Him"*
We were always spending time together leaving the city and just enjoying life, usually in Florida or Atlanta, and going to see his friends - just enjoying each other so much. At five months he surprised me with a ring. He said he just wanted me to know that he loved me and I was not wasting my time with him. I accepted that, and was thinking, "This is really going to work. We are in love and have so much fun together."

We just enjoyed each other's company no matter what we did. I had him stepping out of his comfort zone and doing things he didn't normally do and going places he didn't particularly like, but he tried for me and I appreciated that. Looking back, I realize that I didn't know what he was used to doing and didn't really ask. It just seemed that he didn't have a chance to really enjoy life, so I thought we were showing each other new and different things, and we both enjoyed being out. I think that his military career had a lot to do with him not doing a lot of things, but since he was retired at that point, he was just enjoying life. We were learning from each other and for me that was very special.

Our relationship was awesome. He was actually staying with me, and I didn't mind because I enjoyed him being there. I enjoyed waking up to him every morning. Two and a half years of love, fun and happiness. But then I received an email and everything changed...

## The Email That Changed Everything

One day I got an email. A nasty, direct, hurtful and full-of-hate email. That's the day that changed my life and relationship. This email so was so mean, and it challenged my relationship. It said he was not my man! That

-I was not the only one he is seeing

-he was using me

-I should be ashamed for letting him live in my house around my kids

-I'm ugly

-I look like a transvestite

-The person he was messing with works with me.

And on it went. With a bit of digging, I found out who sent that email. And yes, I still have that one, and the ones that followed to this day. Technology has really changed so you can find what you need if you're looking. Here's a little advice: when setting up a bogus email, don't use your real name. People can look you up, get your address, Google you and see where you live.

## *Who Was She?*

The person who sent the email was not the person he was involved with, but a friend of "hers". I was hot! The friend needed to mind her business. She put herself into a situation with someone she did not even know; this had nothing to do with her. When I refused to respond and be provoked by this round of drama, she called my house. At first, she pretended to be someone else, but when I refused engage with her, she got so upset while cursing me out that she actually gave me her name. So I looked her up, found out who she was through Facebook, and put it all together.

I had only seen "her" once. The only reason I noticed her then was because I spoke to her in casual greeting, she gave me this look like she hated me. It was such a nasty look, full of ire that it bothered me to the point that I later mentioned it to a friend. I said jokingly to my friend, "I spoke to this lady today and she looked liked she hated me or wanted to knock me out." It was only later that I would find out she was the one who would bring so much chaos and pain into my life.

## *Getting to Know the Real "Him"*

The email really changed my relationship with "him" because this is the first time he lied to me. He told me he couldn't find out who sent the bogus email. Yet he works in IT. So I was confronted with an uncomfortable truth: I was able to find out who sent the bogus email and have very limited tech skills, yet he said he couldn't find the origins and makes his living in tech. At that moment I knew there was something to this situation, that it wasn't some "crazy lady" making up some "crazy story", and he didn't want me to find out.

Ladies, we have to pay attention to the little signs that are there. The ones we tend to overlook because we are so into that man and relationship. When it falls apart, we think about things that happened and we remember the "little stuff" that didn't seem important, but in the end it was very important. We have women's intuition: pay attention to what he says. One lie has to be followed by another and he has to keep it going. Eventually, he'll get caught in it. I always say, "Why lie?" When you lie, you have to remember what you said, to whom you said it, and under what circumstances. It's too much work to keep up with lies.

## *After the Lies*

I'm not the type of person to do drama. I'm just not into that. But I have to say that if you come for me, be prepared. I'm not going to allow disrespect, so just know you will get it back.

Yet my relationship didn't end immediately. I loved this man. I was not going to allow some side chick to break up my relationship. He and I had a discussion about this and I asked him, "Why didn't you tell me?" and responded that she was someone that he had been messing with for about five years while he was married. He also said that he was deployed for most of that time and it was never a relationship. I don't know. I wasn't there and it had nothing to do with me. Everyone has a past and if that's what she was, then that's where she needed to stay. I was in love with him and I was not going to allow anyone to dictate who I could and could not be with.

But I have to step out here and say this: if you are messing with someone's husband and when he finally gets a divorce and he doesn't commit to you, and goes and starts another relationship with someone else - what does that say?! I think it says he was not into you like that! Ladies, we are treated the way we allow men to treat us. If you date a man and he does not take you out in public, trust me, there is a reason. If he is meeting your family and you're not meeting his, there is a problem. He may introduce you to a sister, cousin or friend who "knows how he is", but the important people in his life you will not meet.

Boundaries must be set. You must be honest, and communication is very important. And you have to trust until you are given a reason not to, otherwise you will just run him away. No person wants to constantly hear complaining or nagging or drama when there really is none. There is nothing attractive about that. Remember: all men don't cheat. Sometimes, there really is a woman who wants what you have and will do whatever she can to get it. I think the key to any relationship is communication and honesty. When you have a problem, talk about it. Always be open and honest with your mate. Every woman wants a good man and every man wants a good woman.

*The Drama*

As I stated earlier; my relationship didn't end with this drama, but I have to admit that this drama affected my relationship and it eventually did end. Drama caused anger, resentment, and eventually killed the trust. It was very hurtful when he left. I had to deal with the drama on a daily basis. I saw what was going on. I heard the lies being told on me. I saw the people driving by my house taking pictures of "his" car in my driveway.  I told him what was going on and I don't think he believed me or didn't care. The right thing to do when all this drama started would have been for "him" to pull his side-chick to the side and talk to her. To put "her" in her place and let her know it was over and end the drama.  I didn't do it and refused to do it.  It wasn't that I had a problem talking to "her", but it was more that I felt that I didn't owe her anything and that it was his place to handle that. I didn't date her, I didn't talk to her and for me she was really a non factor in my life.  She wasn't being a woman about it, she actually acted like child.

The drama went on for a while, and it got to the point where I couldn't take it anymore and neither could he, so he left. My relationship ended because of another woman.  Wow. She didn't want me with him and in the end, he gave her just what she wanted. I could not believe this was happening to me, but it was and I had to accept it.

*Aftermath*

When he first packed up and left, I let him go. I had dealt with drama on a daily basis and he just left. There were many situations she instigated outside of the phone calls and emails.

I dealt with so much unnecessary drama it took a toll on me. But through all of that, I remained in character. It's just who I am. I will not show any hurt or pain. I kept functioning on a daily basis at work, but when I came home I was just a mess. My bedroom became my comfort zone. I was feeling like I had been mistreated, disrespected, and betrayed. I had done nothing but fall in love. Love is not supposed to hurt. Love is supposed to feel good, comfort, and make you happy. I was far from happy.

Remaining in character was difficult at times, but I had to because I respected myself. I'm a mother and grandmother. I've always taught my children that your reactions to drama and mess can carry consequences. I tell them constantly to "think before you react no matter how hard it is". It takes only a minute to react and things can turn into a bad situation in an instant that can take a long time to get out of.

Although I was brutally hurt by this situation, I am better for it. I've become stronger and wiser. And I realized since he walked out instead of standing and fight that he was not the one for me. Apparently, he wasn't the one for "her" either: even after leaving me, I heard through the grapevine that he did not go back to "her".

I'm moving forward in life. And it's been a difficult journey. But what I once thought was impossible is just a process to get through, get pass, and get over.

# Forgive, Forget, Forward

I have something that I call the Three F's of life: forgive, forget, and forward.

**Forgive**: you have to forgive the person who has wronged you. Not just for you, but because it's the right thing to do.

Forgiving is very hard. I had to pray and repent, fast, mediate, cry, and repeat. I've done it all to be able to be set free from holding on to the bitterness that came from the relationship with "him". I learned that while I was holding on to bitterness, he had moved on, was enjoying life and probably not thinking of me, the pain I'd endured or what I was doing.

**Forget**: you have to learn to forget the person who wronged you. It's hard enough letting go of bitterness, but once you occupy your time with positive, motivational activities, then you will eventually forget about the person or situation that has you tied down.

Forgetting is hard. It's a process that takes as long as it takes, but eventually you will forget about all of "this". I'm at a place now where I can say that the person who has hurt me has been forgiven, and I don't really think about all the pain I've endured. I just focus on the good things I have going on and enjoy my life. I will never forget him, but I will forget all the things that were done to me. My life is still going on, day after day, and so is his. So if he has forgotten about me, I should be doing the same.

I'm going through that process. Nothing will happen overnight, but it will happen. There was a very low point in my life where my room became my comfort zone and I didn't want to go anywhere or be with anyone. That was a sign of depression. After becoming fed up with being tired and stressed, I was forced to think about life and what was next. I had to think about what my life was going to be, my future. I came to realize that my life was a gift from GOD and I didn't want to waste any of it just lying around every day.

It was a process for me. Music has always relaxed me, so I found that listening to music helped. Going for a scenic drive helped, too. I also love to read, so I took my Kindle to the park and read. The last two things were a good start for me, because I removed myself from my bedroom (the comfort zone) and got out of the house. Find something that you like to do and do it. Enjoy life and have fun. Working out, and also walking and listening to my music helped me refocus and relieved a lot of stress.

This brings me to my last F. **Forward**: moving forward in life. Forward is about moving on and doing things better than before.

First, focus and work on yourself so you that you will develop into a better person who is well prepared for life's next chapter. When moving forward, think about what you want out of life. Think about what you want from your partner. List all the qualities you're looking for and be intentional about finding them in your mate. Don't settle, and never go into a relationship just because the other person wants to be with you. Be honest with yourself and the other person. I've come across men who have tried to talk to or date me, but if they didn't have the qualities I was looking for, then did not lead them on. I believe in honesty and if you're really not interested in the person, don't give out your number or even enter into a deep conversation with him. I know that last one sounds harsh, but sometimes when we entertain a conversation with someone who we already know we will not give a chance, we wind up settling for and putting up with the very things we said we would not just so we have something to do.

# Living in Singleness

I've been single for over three years now. I have dated, but I have not committed to any relationship. I'm just enjoying life. I'm working on me and figuring out what I want out of life. While you're living in singleness, this is the best time to work on you. I've learned that all of my relationships ended because none of the men were the man God designed for me. They were NOT my husband. GOD has a plan for me and for my life and it did not include anyone who lied, cheated or walked out of my life. So I'm single and I wait.

### *Comfort in Singleness*

When I first started going places single, with others and couples, I felt a little odd. It made me feel that people were talking about me or saying things like "what's wrong with her that she doesn't have a man"? But I had to stop worrying about what others were saying or thinking about me and stay with what I believed in: not settling. I came to that realization during a time when I did not have a male friend I wanted to bring around this group of couples because I did not want to give the impression that I was in a relationship, so I just always went alone. And the group was very welcoming, even in my singleness, so I felt comfortable hanging out alone with them.

I'm the type of person that if I bring a man around friends or family, then it's serious (unless we are just really good friends and hang out a lot together). But I don't have anyone in my life like that. I have male associates, and a few I consider friends, but those men are in committed relationships. I respect that and would never do anything to cause drama for them.

### *Good Character*

The Webster's definition of character is "the way someone thinks, feels, and behaves; someone's personality. A set of qualities that are shared by many people in a group, country, etc. A set of qualities that make a place or thing different from other places or things."

Be of good character - always. Your character is you. It's who you are, how you carry yourself, and how you conduct yourself around others. Your first impression of someone is based largely on their character. Your character is built over a lifetime, and will be with you always - it's who you are.

I do believe people can change, but sometimes the choices we make in life will haunt us later. And that's why I said earlier I had to thank my dad, because if I was hanging out with my friends and doing some of the things most have done at an early age, I wouldn't want to even image how people would perceive me now as an adult. It does follow you when you are living in the same place you were raised. It's hard to let that go. So I've always carried myself as a lady and that's how I'm treated. I don't tolerate or allow disrespect.

I have to admit that while I embrace a positive demeanor now, my attitude hasn't always been the best. I remember my dad telling me when I was a teenager. "Looks are not everything but your attitude is". I had a very bad attitude and I think it was because I was so mean growing up. I heard it but, I didn't really pay much attention to it. But once you become an adult, you start to evaluate things and looking at yourself. When dealing with people in your personal or professional life, your attitude goes a long way. So I adjusted mine. There were really some people who didn't want to be bothered with a nasty attitude. And who can blame them? My nasty attitude got me nowhere.

Aside from my attitude, I have always been a good friend. I don't consider everyone I associate with a friend. I consider them associates. And I'm even a good friend to them. What people don't know about me is that I really don't like drama.

I don't talk about people behind their backs. If I have something to say about that person that's not good, I will keep it to myself. I have discussions and that's a difference. We can discuss things and agree or not. I don't like drama even though I had a lot surrounding me the last five-and-a-half years. I just feel if you have a problem with someone then you should address it with that person. Or don't be bothered with them at all. Let it go, and keep things moving. No need for drama or stress, the only thing it does is wear you down and interfere with your health. It's not worth it.

*Self-Care*
When your relationship has ended, you must take time for yourself. This is the time when you plan the next chapter of your life. This was a very hard time for me because I spent so much time planning things around my ex and our relationship. It was so hard for me to see myself with someone other than him. So, thinking about a future without "him" was almost impossible.

The end of a relationship is a loss, and we should treat it as such, including respecting the grieving process. When my relationship with "him" ended, I didn't think about it in those terms until I saw a counselor. After telling him my story, he asked me if I had taken time to grieve. I said, "No, I've been so hurt by the breakup and I have things to take care of so I have to keep moving." I then realized he was right. The breakup was a loss and needed to be grieved. The relationship went on for so many years and it was cutting my heart so deep to let go, so I hadn't moved on or let go. So I gave myself permission to grieve - to cry, to yell, to be quiet, and to pray.

This is the point where I realized that I was a selfish prayer. I was praying for GOD to bring "him" back to me and to let him love me and me only, and to let us make it work. And God did answer my prayers: God sent "him" back to me, many times, off and on - from three days to two weeks at a time. Each time, he went back to doing the same things that broke us apart.

It took me a long time and plenty of research, reading many books and Goggling information on the internet so see what others were going through and how they dealt with a breakup. I knew I needed help because this breakup was like no other. I couldn't bear my life without "him". All the plans we made and his promises... this was not supposed to happen, but it did. He betrayed me by walking out.

My hurt and pain went on for over three and a half years. While this person was living his life, having fun and doing whatever with a smile on his face and I just existed, doing what I had to do to get by... Fake-smiling, fake-laughing and just getting through each day. I sometimes would sit at work with tears coming down my face, just so depressed and hiding it from others. I was really going through it. I'd frequently ask myself what I did to anyone in my life to have to endure such pain. I couldn't think of anything. I wasn't a bad child. I wasn't a disrespectful person who just mistreated people. I've always believed in treating others the way I wanted to be treated, and I just felt like I was being punished and had no idea for what.

Now, I'm also the type of person who, if you crossed me or came for me, I would put you in your place and be done with you. If I didn't dish it out, then I don't think it should be coming for me. But my break up didn't originate with any situation like that.

My kids never knew what I was going through. I shielded that from them because he had been in my life so long. I didn't think they needed to know or be in adult relationships or business. I also felt that if people knew what I was going through (including my family and people who were somewhat close to me), they would judge me as being weak and stupid.

I've always been a strong person. But I was just completely shut down because I loved a man more than I loved myself. And I did. I thought he was perfect. I thought we were the perfect couple. We were the black Barbie and Ken.

Looking back it's just crazy now thinking about how much love I gave to this man, and didn't receive the same in return. A part of me hurts to write that I ever loved another more than I loved myself.

*Looking Back*

I have dealt with so much pain. Pain I thought I could never get over. I felt that I was done wrong and this person was my husband, he was the man GOD had designed for me. He walked out and I begged him more than once not to leave me. This was a very difficult time for me. I hurt so bad there were times when I didn't want to leave my bed, my room or my house. I was just going to work and home. Sometimes I couldn't eat or think. I remember going to work and just coming home. I didn't want to socialize with anyone. It hurt. My self-esteem was at the lowest point, and I had to keep going. I was just hoping and praying he would call me and make things right. And you know what? He did. I became his whenever he wanted me. And I went along with this for years and yes, he kept promising we would get back together and promised that I would be the one he marries. He even proposed to me, on one knee with a ring.
I was surprised because we had been going through so much back and forth and drama. But I gave him another chance thinking if he's doing this he's ready. It never happened, and it's not going to happen. I had allowed this person to use, disrespect, lie, cheat and anything else you can think of because I thought he was the one, but he was only a liar and using me for the moment.

Coming to that realization hit me hard. I felt it set me back to the beginning with all the pain I had endured when he first left. It was the beginning of the process of getting over this broken promise and letting this man go. I had to completely get him out of my system so I could put my life back together. I was living a lie, like I had this relationship that was so good in front of everyone else, but inside it was killing me. Stressing me out because I put on this face for everyone else that we were happy and the best couple in the world. It was all a lie. I invested four years into something that was only meant to last two-and-a-half years. What I know now is that if a man walks out of your life he is not the man GOD designed for you. Please understand that he only wants you at his connivance.

*Confronting Self*

Looking back, the day I received that crazy email was the day I should have cut "him" off completely. If I knew then what I know now, I would have done that. "Hind sight is 20/20 as the elders used to say."

"His" rejection was so hurtful that when another man tried to talk to me or get to know me, I would push him away. I realize that I have hurt men along the way to my own healing, and for that I am so sorry. I knew I was not ready to entertain another relationship, but I tried to date and tried to show interest, but I just wasn't ready. So, I actually played with these men feelings and turned out to be no better than "him": I was doing the exact same thing to others as he had done to me. The only difference was that I never committed to a relationship because I knew I was a broken woman.

I apologized to the people I hurt - I had to. I should have never entertained them while I was going through all of that. I never meant to hurt anyone or make them think that all women are hardened. I regret that I made someone very cautious for the next woman because someone did it to me. It's a cycle. And that's why I say please work on you before moving on.

I also realize that there is nothing that I have been through that wasn't a life lesson. I've learned from all the hurt and pain. Nothing I've been through shall be wasted. It's making me a better and stronger person each day for my next chapter.

# Would Have, Should Have, Could Have

Would I have let "him" go if I had known how he was before we got together? Maybe.

Should I have let "him" go when he started to change? Maybe.

Could I have let "him" go when the change was obvious? Maybe.

I answered "maybe" to all of these questions because it's the truth. When your heart hurts because of the love you have for someone, it's easier said than done to let him go, so you have to learn from what has happened to you and move on. Life has no "do overs".

I've learned from reading books and listening to sermons that our lives have purpose, and if a person is no longer in your life, she/he has served his/her time and given you important information you need to move on to your next stage in life. She/he was with us for a season and a reason. The season is just the amount of time invested in the relationship; the reason... well, sometimes it takes a while for that make itself clear, but it will be revealed eventually. And when it is, you will be a much better person for it.

There are things I've done in my life that I regret, including relationships. But I've learned that I
-should work on myself
-could have made better choices
-if I had taken time to heal, I would have been a better person a lot sooner than later.

But there's no better time than now to get things together and enjoy life.

Because of "would have, should have and could have," I realized that I have to love myself before I can love anyone else. I cannot give myself to someone and say that I love them unless I love me first.

Today I can honestly say I do love me.

The man you meet, the one who is for you will see that in you. I can't speak for a man, but I do believe that men sense when we are confident and when we are vulnerable. That knowledge can be used against us: good or bad, right or wrong.

We are all designed to be different. If we were all the same size, had the same eyes, shape, or hair, there would be no room for choices. We are uniquely made to give men a choice of a woman, and men are made different so we can have choices as well.

When you love yourself you have confidence, and it shows. It doesn't mean you have to be a certain size or look a certain way, as long as you are happy when you look in the mirror that's what matters.

Love you and you will be able to love someone else. Take time for you, and treat yourself like you are the best thing walking because you are. Now if you don't feel that way, then you need to start looking at what you don't like about yourself and work on that. Having a nice personality, treating others as you want to be treated, giving someone a smile or even a hello goes a long way. You never know what others are going through.

As women, our standards and quality-of-life should be of the highest caliber.
We are all unique women in our own ways. We are beautifully made and have characteristics and qualities that are unique. They are our own. We possess them, were born

with them, and use them in our daily lives. GOD only made one of each of us, only one of YOU.

Dealing with a breakup can affects us in many ways: physically, emotionally, and mentally. We have to know that GOD has designed a man for each of us and it's not necessarily the person who we think or want it to be. Sometimes we find a man who is nice, attractive and treats us like we are a queen, and then he leaves. He just walks out. Why? Only he knows. Sometimes we won't understand until we meet the man who's designed for us.

People are put into our paths at various times and we can learn from different situations. It's not an easy task, but I have found that through prayer anything is possible. Dealing with a breakup is a very tough time for women and men, especially if cheating was involved. Now, in my personal opinion and it's my opinion only, I think if someone cheats on you and you give them a pass without consequences, it will happen again. This is from my personal experience. I've had this to happen several times. I had to finally let it go. I forgave the first time; but when it happened again and again, it was time to go. No one deserves that.

So many times I watch talk shows and they bring their significant other onto the show for a lie detector test or to confront them for cheating. The majority of the time the person already knew before they got there that it was going on. And sometimes they have even forgiven their significant other for the cheating once or twice before, but there were no consequences. By this time that person thinks you are weak and needy and they can treat you like you are nothing. Here this: you are EVERYTHING, and have so much worth, so please never let anyone tell you you're not!

I have been cheated on, lied to and hurt in ways I thought I would never be able to get over, but there are ways to help deal with a break up and it takes time. Remember this: if you go on to the next man, then you're probably in it for the wrong reasons. You have to take some time for yourself, to get to know you! Take some time to figure out what you want out of life, how you feel about yourself, and what you expect when you start dating again. This was a lonely process for me, but I did it during the winter months, so it was a good time to work on me. Reading, praying, fasting, meditating and listening to sermons helped me in so many ways - and continue to help.

A cheater will cheat, a liar will lie, and a player will play. We can only change ourselves. Once we do, hopefully we will attract a true and kind man who is only interested in us. There is someone out there for everyone and sometimes we just have to wait.

Live in singleness. It's truly a blessing and it give you time for yourself. You will grow and learn during this time. You will appreciate the fact that you've done this. You should find hobbies, and read to exercise your mind and body. Work on the things about yourself you want to improve. Learn new things. Take a trip, and most importantly enjoy yourself. Singleness is a gift from GOD. So put Him first and date Him. Read His word. Learn His will, plan and purpose for your life. He will reveal all to you in time.

As a single woman, I've often said it's hard to find a good man, but there are men who feel the same way about women. I think that if we take time to work on ourselves and love ourselves and prepare ourselves for when the right person comes along, then we will know and be prepared for the next chapter.

We all have standards - as we should. Personally, I'm not willing to settle for less than my standards just to say I have someone - that would not be fair to me or the person I'm dating.

Sometimes we can get so caught up on the material things that we miss out on the important things. Ladies, always want a man who respects you, is able to provide for you, and will protect you and profess his love for you. This is straight out of Steve Harvey's book. Anyone can have a man, but you want the right man for you.

Be willing to be objectively critical: analyze the man by comparing him to your standards list - within reason. For instance, if a man is not as tall as I like, but has a good attitude and personality, and treats me with respect, he may win me over.

Now I'm not saying no one is good enough for me. That's far from the truth. I'm just willing to be honest about what I want, what I will accept, and what I won't deal with.

There is a difference between settling for and making adjustments to the qualities you desire. Personality, attitude, and mannerism are a big "musts" for me and I'm not willing to settle for or adjust on these things. But I will adjust my desires on outward appearance, such as height. Don't get me wrong: I love looking up at a tall man, but I'm willing to meet him eye to eye if there is a connection and he treats me right.

Just think about this: which would you rather have? A man who
-treats you right, is very respectful to you, your family and your friends, is everything you could imagine, works (but doesn't make as much money as you do), does things with you and for you.
OR
-makes a lot of money, treats and talks to you like you're nobody, sees you when he wants to see you, gives you a few dollars to keep you "happy", and does what he wants when he wants to, and with whom he wants.

Just something to think about! Sometimes money can cause us to choose the wrong relationship. I just want a man who is financially secure so that I'm not taking care of him.

# Dumping

We all like to share (AKA dump) our problems onto others, and it's okay if you are really open to hear criticism and/or the truth. Everyone is not going to agree with your way of thinking and how you do or deal with things and it's okay - that's a part of life. However, I do want to let you know that dumping can also cause problems in your relationships.

For example, if you're in a relationship and you are having problems, you may decide to go dump on your family. Be very careful with this: sometimes family may not be as forgiving as you are. They are only hearing what you're telling them and while there are two sides to every story, if you are angry you are really talking too much. Sometimes it's best to calm down before we talk to anyone about the situation.

Everyone has their opinion about things so when you ask, be ready for some constructive criticism or an opinion, and it may not be what you want to hear. I've had friends to come to me and ask my opinion about something and the next thing you know they have an attitude because I didn't agree with them and how they saw things.

Ladies, let me say this: some things are best unsaid. Just keep it to yourself. You don't have to put all your business out for everyone to know.

The thing that happens when we are dumping our problems on others is judgment comes in. And usually when it's family and someone has hurt you, they have very strong opinions about this. It usually involves you leaving this person alone or they are no longer welcomed around them. So you have to be very careful. You may get back together and because you have dumped this information out there, your family and friends may not want to be bothered with this person any longer, and can't understand why you want to go back to that person. But your heart is so into it you don't want to let the person go. So now when you have family gatherings and he is with you, it's an odd situation for all.

We have all "dumped" at one time or another in our lives, however the point I'm trying to make is when you are putting friends and family into your personal situation, judgment comes. For example: a family member who is married had an argument with his wife. She was already stressed out and going through some things. Now she gets upset and shows her firearm. She showed it to make a point to this person (of course that's not the way to handle any situation, especially when you're angry). Now, when this is mentioned to the family, it makes everyone look at that relationship differently. Everyone had their say and opinion about the situation and told him to leave her... but that's easier said than done. He left for a couple of days, but he loved her so he went back and forgave her. Trust me when I say the family was not so forgiving. They talked about kicking her butt, but out of respect for him, did not get involved.

Situations like this can get messy and you have to make sure you are prepared for the repercussions when you are dumping things on family. The risk is that your family will never look at the person the same way, and only tolerate him/her for your sake.

Sometimes, you may decide to dump because you want someone to be aware of what's going on, just in case something happens. That's not a bad idea, but it needs to be handled in a certain way. Know who you can trust to keep your secret and don't tell the entire family unless it's absolutely necessary to get them involved.

When dumping, there are some family and friends you have to give the disclaimer "this is just my opinion…" I often have friends ask me what I think about certain things and even though I give the disclaimer, things still get a bit dicey.

I have this friend who is always talking to me about things going on and asking my opinion about different things. When it comes to discussing men, this is where the disconnect or disagreements usually come. To keep the discord to a minimum, I usually reply, "A man will respect you if you have some type of standards." Ladies, if you meet guys online they can tell you anything. I would listen to my friend's stories and think to myself, "Are you really older than me?!" Some of the things she'd say were just ridiculous. For instance, she would give her personal contact information after one online encounter. I would never meet a guy online and immediately give him my personal information. You can't tell a guy where you live and invite him to your home after one online encounter! You have to get to know a person by communicating - online, then move to the phone, and see how things go from there.

Be patient ladies. Patience is good and will be rewarded. When it's time to meet, make sure it's in a public place. My poor friend would tell her story and I would hear things that sound beyond farfetched… She'd believe anything the man said, no matter how outlandish or outrageous. My only response could be, "How do you know it's true?" I had to limit my responses because I didn't want to say anything to hurt her feelings because I'm a good friend and listener… but

I was dying inside.

I have heard story after story of women meeting men, seeing them, and the situations immediately go to sex. Why? Because sometimes we put it out there. If a guy starts talking to you like that within 30 minutes or so of meeting you that's all on his mind. If you take the bait, then he is going to run with it. He is not wanting to get to know you personally, he is just out to get what he can from you. He may call you again, but it's only for a booty call. He will never date you. You will not meet his family or friends. He will only see you when he wants to see you for that "one thing". Trust me, there will never be a relationship. I've tried to explain this to another friend over and over again. I don't see why she allows men to treat her like that, especially when she's getting absolutely nothing out of it - except hurt feelings. I know she wants a relationship because she has said many times she is tired of being alone. But you have to go about it in the right way, have self- respect and a little patience to attract the right man.

My girlfriend and I are still friends today, but I try not to go there with her on the man talk because it's always the same thing: this guy, that guy and still meeting people online. I've told her before to write down the type of man she wants - from his height to his weight and all the qualities she would like for him to have. And if that's the type of man she wants, then she has to first work on herself to ensure she's ready for that type of man. I think that you have to deal with yourself and your own personal issues before you can find the man you want. Trust me: there is someone out there for everyone - including YOU.

I have more sympathy and empathy for my friend than it appears in the above paragraphs. She was really hurt by her ex-husband. When a man leaves you for another woman that can be devastating; it will have you questioning yourself about what you did or didn't do, how you look and dress, and you may even compare yourself to the other person.

NEWS FLASH: Don't do it! When a man hurts us, it really hurts, but that man left because he wanted something else - period. You are not the first woman to be cheated on and you will not be the last. Don't take that man's leaving as a referendum on your character or looks.

I know: we cry and we can't figure out why "this" is happening to us. I've been there and done that, too, - more than once. But ladies, let me just say that when you are hurt by someone, learn from it. Take some "you time" and get yourself together. That's where living in singleness comes in. Use it as a time for self-improvement. In my friend's case, I feel she used her body and slept with these men for a few minutes of attention, and when it was over, the man was gone and she was feeling bad because there was another one who did the same thing: "He slept with me and now he's gone." But you have to own your part of it. You allowed it. You entertained the conversation and he knew he could have you "just like that".

Your body is precious and you should treasure it. You should give it to a man you are in a committed relationship with and care about. Treasure that and if it doesn't work out, then learn from it, and work on self again until you're ready find someone else. But always have some standards. And never allow any man to disrespect you.

I'm here to listen when my friend is hurting and I will continue to do so. I just hope the light bulb will come on and she will say… "Ok, I got it". If this is you, you have a person in your life who loves you and cares about you - but you have to listen to him/her. Hopefully, you'll come around and say, "I'm going to try it your way and see if I can meet a nice man who wants me for me and to be in a committed relationship." But this can only happen when you decide to work on yourself and confront head on the self-esteem issues that lie there.

Having strong, positive self-esteem is so important. You have to feel good about yourself because it shows when you don't, the wrong type of man who will pick up on it and use it to his advantage. Not all men - *the wrong type of man* - the man you <u>don't</u> want. There are some really good men out there. It's just a matter of meeting the one that's right for you. The first step in meeting that man is to feel good about yourself and letting him know it.

When we solicit someone's opinion, we should listen and process it in love - i.e., not take it the wrong way. Besides, you are going to do things the way you want anyway! (That's what my friend does.) Just know that eventually, you'll meet the right one, only after you leave alone the ones who are only after "one thing" or in a relationship with someone else. If he has someone and is cheating with you, then he would probably do the same to you.

I hope that my experiences and the things I've seen over the years will truly help you to move forward because I can promise you that the pain will go away. It's not an overnight process and it's not impossible. It can be done.

# Are There Warning Signs?

Are there always warning signs or red flags? Usually. If I had paid attention, I would have saved myself a lot of anger, pain, resentment, bitterness, frustration. Signs were there during the relationship and I just ignored them. That happens when we are in a relationship. We sometimes lose our selves in the relationship, even when we know and see other things going on around us, but we tend to send them to the "backseat".

For me, the warning was lying about simple things. And yes, there were times when I would think, "Didn't he tell me something else?" That was the first sign. For example, I remember a time when he told me a story about his family and his grandmother who raised him. He also told me how they had the house torn down because of the memories. Then when I went to Florida, he showed me the house. Yes, I thought about this lie, but did I call him out on it? No, I just let it go. There were other stories about his family, and once I met them later, found that what he told me was totally different.

The point I'm trying to make is that in my pervious relationship, he started off doing things I liked to get my attention and to prove to me that he really wanted to be with me. Once the relationship started to get old and he was sure I was in love, the changes started coming: he didn't like walks in the park, he only took them because I liked them. Once he "had me", the walks stopped.

The first two years we dated, there was never a time I called his phone and he did not answer. Never! He would answer on the golf course... But suddenly, all of that changed and that was another warning sign.

When I noticed changes in his behavior, when he all of a

sudden needed to be away more, I really didn't pay attention because I trusted him. I didn't question it, I just let it go. But it turns out that was another warning sign that I chose to ignore.

Then came a time I called and he would not answer. And now all of a sudden, he had to work late and weekends.

He started going out of town more often, saying it was for his job or that he had to go home to Florida, but didn't want me to go. All of these instances were signs of trouble that I ignored and now that the relationship is over, I realize what was going on.

When a man starts changing certain habits, you take notice, but do you necessarily say anything? He may suddenly like wearing colorful underwear, which he never wanted to do before - not the *bright* colors. And he may suddenly want to work out, yet you couldn't get him to do that before.

It's interesting: he could have just told me if he was tired of the relationship and wanted out. I would rather take that hurt and pain than all the other that I endured. And the worst thing, besides cheating, is lying. Once a liar, always a liar: you have to continue the lie until the end. And when you lie on family and close friends, you really have some issues. I have to admit my "women's intuition" went off many times, but I chose to ignore it. I was in love.

Pay attention to everything, but don't get to the point where you are accusing your significant other all the time and losing focus of what's important - your relationship. Trust is key to any relationship. If you love him, you have to trust him, but if the changes come, pay attention.

I am strong woman, but I know that even as strong women we get caught up and get hurt - that is why I'm writing this book, to help someone deal with these things.

# Woman to Woman

Why do women go after the "other woman"? I don't understand women who do this. Unless it's a family member or close friend who is aware of your relationship, why go after the other person who you feel is messing it up?

We have to understand that the other person does not owe us any explanation. They don't! The person you are in a relationship with who has betrayed you does. This happens all the time. And often times it leads to someone getting hurt - emotionally and physically.

I have been in situations where I've been cheated on. But I never went after the other person. Why would I? I've dealt with the person who cheated on me. There has only been one time in my life that I have done that and that's because she was a longtime friend and she betrayed me. I did not get violent with her because she is not worth me getting charged with a felony. This is where we have to think before we react. I simply let my ex-friend know that she was so wrong on every level and to stay out of my presence. I told her, "Since you know me so well you know I don't play that." And I did let her know I would kick her butt. But here's the thing: he also betrayed me. So if I forgave him, shouldn't I forgave her? That was a hard thing to do, but I did. I forgave both of them because it was the right thing to do. Now this did not happen overnight, but it did happen. Of course I left the relationship, and it was a process, but I was able to move FORWARD.

I have since seen my former friend, made small talk with her, and kept it moving. Forgiveness does not mean you have to deal with that person. It just means the situation is over and you no longer discuss it. She and I will never be friends again because I don't need friends like that - one betrayal is enough.

There are often too many stories that many times end in disaster that are associated with "a relationship gone wrong". Why do we involve people who have nothing to do with each other in messy or uncomfortable situations? If you are in a relationship and it's not working, the best thing to do is to explain to the other person why you're not happy. No need to involve anybody else in the situation. Just end the relationship and keep it moving. Try to make it as simple as possible, without any extra drama. Everyone involved is not a cheater or liar, particularly the "other" person. Problems come when innocent people (many times that "other person") are involved in an unknown love triangle - and often times someone gets hurt or even killed.

Now that's some serious drama, but it does happen. Is lying worth someone dying for? I don't think it is. Be honest, be an adult, communicate, and move on. Violence never ends well and it definitely doesn't solve problems.

The question for me is why do women go after the other woman when it was their man who cheated? I don't understand this. Of course this has happened to me. If I had known he was in a relationship, I wouldn't have been with him. And if he was in a relationship with this person, where was she when he and I were constantly out with his family and friends all over the city and out of town - almost every weekend? But, oh, it's my fault?! I don't think so.

And yet she was very upset at me. She accused me of taking her man. She dogged me out on my job to others, and she had someone send to me threatening emails and make threatening phone calls to my home phone.
The person I am today won't entertain drama - I can't. I'm in a different place in my life. I've grown spiritually and

cannot allow anyone to take that away. Now, that doesn't mean I'm a push over; I stand for what I believe in and I'm still a work in progress. I just try to stay focused on the important things in life and let the childish behavior and drama fall by the wayside.

# Rejection

No woman likes to be rejected, no matter who it's from, but especially not by a man. I put it into perspective and keep it moving with this realization: people like what they like. Men know the type of woman they want, just like we women know the type of men we like. Ladies, don't ever date someone just because he wants to date you. Always maintain your standards and requirements.

But what happens when a man you want doesn't want you? Ladies, try not to take rejection as a bad thing. I've been rejected many times, and it's happened to me while writing this book. I had a friend who insisted I meet this person, who actually turned out to be very nice... but he didn't like me "like that". One day he will make someone a good husband - just not me.

As of the writing of this book, I'm not ready to be in a relationship, but I'm definitely getting there. Maybe by the time the book is published I will be. Don't push yourself to be ready for something new; it will come naturally. I know from experience: I tried going into a relationship when I knew I wasn't ready, just to appease a friend. I wasn't feeling it, but went along with it anyway and it didn't end well.

I've found the hardest rejection to process is that which comes out of nowhere. If a person shows some interest in me and then just stops without an explanation, I want to know if I did something or said something to offend him. I actually ask so I may use that information for future reference. But if no explanation can be obtained, then I know it may be that he was really not interested in me - or had someone else.

I've had someone dump me for no reason, and to this day still don't know why. He and I dated many years ago when I was in my early 20's. He was in the military and deployed during Operation Desert Storm. I was here in the States and yes, I waited for him. There was no reason to believe the relationship would end badly: we were cool. We'd been friends for a year before we decided to date. It was not too long after we decided to date that he found out he was being deployed. So while he was gone, we wrote a lot and he would call. He also had his sister, whom I had never met, to call and check on me. I thought, "This man really likes me if he is doing this."

When he came back State side, I was there when the plane landed. It was raining hard that day, but I was there to meet him. I took him back with me and we spent the next couple of days together, before he even went to see his family.

The day before he was to leave, we went to lunch, came back to the house and he told me he no longer wanted to be with me. Just like that. I was confused. I asked why and he said, "I don't know. I just can't." I was confused and hurt by this, and from that day forward I'd never dated any man on active duty. Looking back, it's sad because I may have really met someone who would have been a good partner, but that's the way it is.

Since then, I've regretted some of my dating choices. Honestly, when I look back at some of them, I just don't know what I was thinking. Sometimes, I think we can be in a zone where we are living and doing things without caring or thinking. I've done this more than once. But today, since I know what type of man I desire and deserve, I'm willing to wait for him. I'm no longer looking, I'm just waiting because the one for me only will find me when the time is right. How do I know? Because I prayed and asked GOD to send him to me, and I have faith that it will be.

Rejection can be used as a learning tool. I've definitely learned a lot and I'm working on me daily. I've determined that I can't allow the bitterness of a breakup to hinder me from meeting my future husband. When the time is right, we will meet. I don't know when, where or under what circumstances, but it will happen.

I started writing this book over two years ago. I was learning and I still am. It was only recently that I realized that I was rejecting men only to spare their feelings because I knew I wasn't ready... and in turn, men rejected me because of how I behaved, my bad attitude, and my self-esteem issues.

The hardest part about rejection is learning to let go. No matter what caused your relationship to end, you have to let it go. You also have to forgive yourself, as well as the other person. Life is too short to dwell on the past, and no one is promised tomorrow - we must live for today. Let's let go of anger, bitterness, resentment, stress, and jealousy, and commit to enjoying life. We only have one life, so why not be happy in it. Enjoy every day like it's your last. It has taken me a very long time - three years - to completely say that I'm a much better person. There was a time I thought I would never get over the hurt and pain of that relationship, but I can honestly say that I have arrived. I'm a better person and I've learned many things along the way. This does not mean I'm immune to future hurt. I hope I don't, but I feel that with all I've gone through I'm a better person to handle it.

During this process, there have been times when I have said that I've forgiven a person, but when put in a situation where I had to face that person, I realized that I had not - the pain was still there. I've been hurt by people who didn't like me for any particular reason and those who didn't like me for whatever personal reason they didn't share with me. I had to learn that either way, it was their problem, not mine; and I had to learn to be okay with that.

I've always been told to treat others as you want to be treated. You never know what someone is going through and we all deal with things. I also had to learn just because a person doesn't "put it all out there" doesn't mean everything is perfect. I just try to give people the benefit of the doubt and move on.

There was a time when there were people I worked with who hated me and I didn't even know why... and when I found out, I was in disbelief: a person in common - who didn't like me - told them lies just to make me look bad. I said a mental "Whatever!" and kept it moving. But I have to admit that I could not help feel annoyed and wonder why grown folks get involved and hate on others when they have nothing to do with a situation? I use to tell my children all the time to "mind your business". There are some grown folks who need to be told the same thing.

We have to stop hating on each other, hurting each other, and just making people feel bad. We should treat others the way we want to be treated - with joy, mercy, and grace.

Once I allowed the relationship to truly end, I never looked back. I started by giving myself 90 days not to date. Once I did that, I gave myself another 90 days. It was a gift to myself, a time to just love me, to build myself back up, to work on Katherine! That work included adjustments to my attitude and my way of thinking.

It also included forgiving people who had lied to me, wronged me and hurt me. You know that you have forgiven someone when you can see them, and you don't react to them. If there's a reaction, then you haven't forgiven them. As long as someone gets a reaction out of you, you are giving them control over how you're feeling when you see them. Let it go!

I have met some amazing people during this journey, and they have really helped me in my growing process - mentally, physically and mostly spiritually. And I thank them from the bottom of my heart.

## What Men Want

Since I'm a single woman, I can't say what a man wants, but I can ask men and I have. The men I've spoken with are what I consider real men. They are very committed to their marriages and relationships. I took the time to ask a few of these real, good men these questions:

- What do our men really want?
- How can I keep my man?
- What have I been doing wrong?
- How do I keep my man happy once the honeymoon is over?

They all agreed on these things:

- They want sex, communication, and consistency.
- The want to keep the fun times going.
- They like their ladies to wear sexy nighties.

These men also said that once women get married they tend to stop doing a lot of the things they did to get their men, and it's hard and frustrating. They also said that with all the temptation out there, it's a challenge to remain faithful. Although these men said that they have not stepped out on their relationships, they also said that they have been tempted many times. So what made these men deny the temptation? A mature relationship with GOD.

One man shared with me that he loves his wife, and even though temptation has crossed his path, he just can't step out on her. He fears GOD and the results. Everything walking and looking cute and attractive is NOT! Every fine thing throwing a smooth line is not good for you! There are too many things out there; one night of passion can cause you a lifetime of pain.

Ladies, we have to step it up. There are so many beautiful women in the world. Once you have the man you've desired, then it's up to you to keep him happy. Now, there are some men who cheat because they can and then say they have an addition. They do not, they just do it because they want to. If a REAL MAN is happy at home - because he knows how his woman takes care of him - he is not going to step out on you. Emphasis on the REAL MAN part!

So how do you keep the fun in the relationship? Continue to do things together. Have a date night. Always smile, laugh and complement each other. Wake that man up at 10:00 pm when the kids are asleep and again at 5:00 am before he goes to work and just show him how much he is appreciated. Send him to work with a smile on his face that says, "I love my woman" and a look in his eye that tells anyone looking, "That woman takes care of her man." Now this is not all about sex. But keeping him focused and happy with you will make a lasting relationship.

Remember to love yourself while you are loving him. Maintain your standards! Love yourself. Know your worth. Know who you are and what you want. Put GOD first in all ways and always. Respect yourself and others. Smile often and laugh when possible. Enjoy life - always.

May you find love and happiness, but know it starts with you.

## Comfort Through Your Pain

When I was going through my worst moments, these aspirations and scriptures really helped me. I hope they do the same for you.

1. The Serenity Prayer. There are many versions of the serenity prayer, but I love and have memorized Reinhold Niebuhr's version.

2. The poem "Hater" by Dr. Maya Angelou.

3. The Bible, Book of Proverbs Chapter 31:10-31 "The Wife of Noble Character".

# The End of My Story

The man that I loved more than anything hurt me to a point that I didn't think I could ever heal from the pain. I kept putting a band aid over the wound, taking it off and putting it back on over and over again. It was three and half years of back and forth betrayal, lies, and hurt. I gave too much of myself to this man, so much that it was hard to recover.

I've dated, met really nice people, but because of my pain and trust issues, I pushed men away. The final end for me in that relationship was when he invited me to his college graduation, then left without me... And when his mom passed on Easter Sunday and he came to me for comfort - which I gave without reservation for two days - he stopped calling me, ignored my calls and text messages. I knew then that it was truly over and there was no point in trying to even consider a relationship and definitely not a friendship.

I have nothing else to say to that person who changed my life but "thank you"! If he hadn't put me through all this, I would have never been able to reach out and help other women who have been through a similar situation. Life goes on. I'm not currently dating. I meet people, but no one who interests me, or the connection is missing.

I've hurt men along the way and of that I'm not proud. There was one in particular, whom I enjoyed being friends with and during a weak time let my flesh have control for a few minutes. That changed the dynamics of our friendship because he wanted to talk about a relationship that I was not ready for. I hate that I treated him wrong because if he had done the same to me, I would have been hurt. I initiated a night of passion and he took it as if we could take it further and I knew that with all that I had dealt with I couldn't and wasn't ready for that. We had been on a few dates and there was a physical connection yet a mental disconnection because I looked at him as someone just to spend time with.

PSA: Ladies, please get yourself together before you mess with the next person, because in the end someone is going to get hurt. Take your time, work on self, and love yourself before you move on.

The last of my pain comes because the betrayal was so deep. I actually saw this person out hanging with his friends, laughing and enjoying life as if nothing had happened... As if he hadn't hurt me.

Through the grace of GOD everything is going to be alright. He says ask and it shall be given. Seek and ye shall find. Knock and the door will be opened.

I hope my story has helped you in a way that will allow you to find the man GOD has designed for you. Always think highly of yourself. You are unique and wonderfully made.

I have let this person back into my life several maybe even close to 20 maybe more after he walked out of my life. I realize now what a mistake that was. But I loved him very much and thought he was my soul mate. It wasn't until I started getting into the WORD, and praying for healing of my broken heart and removal of the pain that I started to see GOD manifest in my life. He brought me out of that relationship. I admit that during the time I was praying, I was asking GOD to bring my man back; and GOD did bring him back to me, but he never stayed. That experience taught me that GOD allows us to have the desires of our hearts, and He answers prayers, but we have to recognize the lesson when it doesn't work out. If there is constant drama, arguments, lying, cheating, or whatever, it's not going to work. For me, the lesson was that man was not the one for me and GOD made me a better person in the process of showing me that.

How? It definitely made me stronger than what I thought I already was. I was taught patience and understanding. I do appreciate the first two years of the relationship and the time we had together. Because of that time, I will never speak badly of him. I saw a part of him that was good, but even realizing that, I know that he is for someone else and I have accepted that. I have also learned to never love a man more than I love myself.

Since coming to that realization, I've opened my mind to empowering books and sermons, some of which had me crying and really made me think about where I was, what I wanted to do and what my purpose in life was. One book that helped me through was Steve Harvey's Act Like A Success, Think Like A Success. It led me to try to understand my life purpose, particularly the question, "What is the one thing you do without the least amount of effort?" I thought about this and had an idea, but I wasn't sure. It was later while listening to a sermon by Bishop TD Jakes that it all came together. Bishop Jakes said, "Nothing you have been through shall be wasted." That really resonated with me, particularly because of all I'd been through. (Please listen to this sermon! It is so powerful and I believe it will change your life and way of thinking for the better, just as it has changed mine.)

Anytime a situation or relationship doesn't work out, there is something to be learned from that experience. The hurt and pain will not be wasted. "Nothing you have been through will be wasted."

I admire both Bishop TD Jakes and Steve Harvey because they just tell the truth about life. Bishop Jakes tells us "how it is" on a spiritual level and Steve Harvey does so on both a spiritual level as well as from a man's perspective - his real-world experiences as to what he's been through and his advice specifically to women to receive the good that is meant for us.

There have been so many times when I've listen to their advice and just felt like they knew exactly what I was going through. TD Jakes sermons have touched me on a spiritual level, to the point where I have transformed my ways and put GOD first. And I love listening to Steve Harvey's radio show, particularly the morning inspirations. They've changed my life. I'm sure those inspirations have changed a lot of lives, and I set my alarm in the morning just so I don't miss a word.

Today I'm in a better place. I'm still growing and learning. I'm living in singleness and enjoying it. I truly hope my story will help you with issues you are having in a relationship. You are not the first and will not be the last to be hurt, mistreated or disrespected. But take your life back, adjust your mindset and live your life to the fullest.

I've done many things in my life, some I'm proud of and some not so much.

BUT THEN GOD! He knew I was hurting so much. He was reaching out to me and I just didn't put it together until I could only pray because of my hurt and pain. This hurt and pain lasted years and I asked Him to remove it. He did! After many days and nights of praying, fasting, and meditating, He led me to a place of worship that has changed my life.

He led me to my church home where I felt so welcomed from day one. My Pastor Bruce O. Alford is an awesome man of GOD. His sermons are so powerful. The first five or six sermons I attended just felt like GOD was speaking directly to me through him. And He really was. I joined the church a year later. I look forward to being there every Sunday. I used to travel on the weekends and stay through

Sunday, but since I've joined this place of worship, I make sure I come home so I can be in church Sunday morning. Finding a church home where you are excited about being "in the place" is a powerful balm for your hurting soul. If GOD can change my life, remove my hurt and pain, and lead me to an awesome place of worship, He can and will do the same for you.

I hope you have enjoyed my story as much as I've enjoyed sharing it with you. Just always show good character and be yourself. If people cannot accept you for who you are, then maybe you don't need them in your life.

People who care about you will never turn their backs on you. I have made some awesome and true friendships. Sometimes you have to change your environment, the people you hang with and the places you go. If you want better, you must do better. You must surround yourself with people who are like you want to be. GOD will help you if you just put your faith to work. Trust GOD always. He sometimes makes us wait to teach us patience. There will be trials and tribulations, but when GOD wants to make you high Quality he makes you wait. There is a plan and purpose for us all, but learn to put GOD first and let Him direct your path.

I'm such a better person today. Give yourself time to heal and grow, and you will be, too. When you're ready to make a decision, just know you are worthy and deserve to be loved by someone who will love you - truly and only you.

I'm still single today. I'm not dating; however, I will go on a date with a male friend. I'm waiting patiently on GOD to reveal to me His purpose. If His plan for me is to be married, then I will wait on my husband and he will find me. I'm enjoying life; developing my spiritual growth and learning each day. I'm truly blessed for all my life lessons. I am sorry for anyone I have hurt along the way, whether intentionally or unintentionally. Life is good and GOD is better.

There is absolutely nothing wrong with singleness. I've actually enjoyed being single. It's a gift from GOD and while you're living in it, date Him and get to know Him. GOD will direct your path, lead you in the right direction, and give you the desires of your heart which will include the man He has designed just for you.

Don't live a confined life. Some relationships, situations, and circumstances can be considered Confined because they cause your life to be filled with bitterness, disappointment, confusion and disbelief. You think you've gotten over the pain and hurt, and that you are ready to move forward, but then it comes again: the pain, hurt, anger, resentment, frustration, bitterness, anxiety and stress rolls in like the tide.

Think about this: if you had to be confined to a room, bed, or wheelchair and GOD gave you the opportunity to move forward and live a life free of this confinement, wouldn't you take it? Of course! You wouldn't willingly stay confined to that room, bed, or wheelchair. Well, that is the pain, hurt, anger, resentment, frustration, bitterness, anxiety and stress that keeps trying to bind and confine you. Let it go!

There will be times in our lives when we are tested, and maybe more than once. If a relationship has confined you with feelings of pain, hurt, resentment, frustration, bitterness, anxiety or stress, then this may not be the relationship for you. If you are just going through the motions of a relationship, and are truly not happy, then you are confined. Let it go!

Live your life to the fullest. Find someone who makes you happy, and puts a smile on your face daily. Stress has a way of breaking our bodies down. We don't really understand the magnitude of stress and I can say this because I've been there and done that. Enjoy every day as if it's your last. No one is promised tomorrow.

Be Blessed Always...

*Katherine D. Carey*

## About the Author

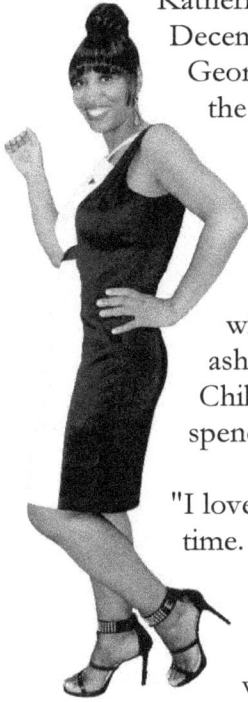

Katherine Carey was born in Waycross, Georgia December 31. She has lived in Columbus, Georgia since she was five years old, and loves the city and its people.

Katherine is the proud and adoring mother to three adult children Keith, Shawn, and Aleshia (Lesi), loves her daughter-in-law Kimberly, and is overjoyed with her grandson Lil Shawn. She is not ashamed of the fact that she spoils her Chihuahua, Prissy Leigh Carey, and loves spending time with family and friends.

"I love enjoying life, taking things one day at a time. I am simply building my life around being a better person than I was yesterday."

To learn more about Katherine, visit her website at www.KatherineDCarey.com.